MORE ERAS: POP PROMPTS FOR SWIFTIES

VOLUME 2

119 WRITING PROMPTS INSPIRED BY THE SONGS OF TAYLOR SWIFT

By Erik Patterson

Camden High Street Books
2024

More Eras: Pop Prompts for Swifties, Volume 2
Copyright © 2024 Erik Patterson

Print ISBN: 979-8-9882250-9-6
eBook ISBN: 978-1-964887-00-5
First Paperback Edition, June 2024

Cover Design by Hannah Alpert
Book Layout by Lydia Godfrey
Copy Editing by Sherry Angel
Printed in the United States of America
Los Angeles, CA

www.erikpatterson.org

This book is meant for educational, scholarship, and research purposes. By taking a critical look at the themes in Taylor Swift's work, we aim to inspire writers to create their own unique works of personal writing and fiction. Writers using this book are encouraged to research their own hearts and psyches in order to become scholars of their inner selves. Song titles are referenced in the spirit of Fair Use and readers should seek out and purchase Taylor Swift's music on their own as a supplement to the original writing prompts in this book. Taylor Swift has no involvement with this book. The use of her name is merely descriptive and should not be interpreted as a sign of endorsement.

Praise for the *Pop Prompts* book series

"If only this book were around when I was getting ready to write *my* book. Erik is the writing docent in your museum of stories and ideas. Read this book and let him help you gather your thoughts and get your mind moving."

—Retta, author of *So Close to Being the Sh*t,*
Y'all Don't Even Know

"Every life is flush with meaningful experiences, and man is it nice to have someone help us excavate them to create. Erik's prompts pick up right where each of Taylor's songs leave off—now it's your turn!"

—Drew Seeley, actor, singer, songwriter

"Turn to any page in *Pop Prompts*, set your timer, and write. Settling in and writing without a plan, I mean truly letting your mind go like Erik advises, is the closest you'll come to God (whether or not you believe)."

—Andrea Askowitz, author of *My Miserable, Lonely,*
Lesbian Pregnancy

"I loved flipping through to my fave Swift songs and getting creatively inspired by the suggestions of how to loosen up my own writing. Whether it's to explore things in your work-in-progress, kick loose stuff in your personal life, or use in a classroom as a warm-up exercise, Erik's playlist prompts help to elevate your writing game."

—Cecil Castellucci, author of *Shifting Earth*

CONTENTS

ALBUM: Midnights

ALBUM: The Tortured Poets Department

7

INTRODUCTION

Let's get one thing out of the way: you don't have to be a tortured poet to use this book.

More Eras: Pop Prompts For Swifties Volume 2 can also be used to inspire novels, screenplays, stage plays, journal entries, and even your own songs. No matter what you write, I expect you to dive into these writing exercises with an inquisitive mind, a sense of joy, and the willingness to be honest with yourself.

These prompts ask you to be vulnerable. One reason we identify with Taylor's music is because she puts her flaws and mistakes out there—we see her interrogating her actions and (most of the time) learning from them. I encourage you to do the same when you're using this book. You don't have to show this writing to anyone else. This writing is for you. See how it feels. If you want to share it with the world, you can decide that later. For now, don't worry what others think: your reputation is not on the line.

Think of this book as your lover. Tell it your secrets. Tell it your own personal folklore.

For those of you who are new to the *Pop Prompts* book series, here's how these writing prompts work:

Every prompt is paired with a song from Taylor's most recent eras: *reputation* (2017), *Lover* (2019), *folklore* (2020), *evermore* (2020), *Midnights* (2022), and *The Tortured Poets Department* (2024). Listen to a song, read the corresponding prompt, then use the "First Thoughts" page to jot down your reaction to the prompt. If you have more to say, use a separate journal.

Happy writing.

MORE ERAS: POP PROMPTS FOR SWIFTIES

VOLUME 2

... *READY FOR IT?*

Do you ever toy with people's feelings?

Everyone wants to think they're not the type who plays emotional games with other people. You could say you always have pure, honest, innocent intentions. But be honest with yourself for a second, and really think about it:

Have you ever been careless with someone else's heart?

Why?

What did you get out of it?

How did it work out?

Write.

FIRST THOUGHTS

END GAME

Do you believe in the idea of a soul mate?

Do you think there's just one person out there who's right for you? What does "right" even mean when it comes to love? How do you know when you've found it?

Where did your ideas about love come from?

What did you learn about love from your parents?
What did you learn about love from your friends?
What did you learn about love from the movies?
What did you learn about love from your own experiences?

How have all these lessons about love shaped who you are?

Write.

FIRST THOUGHTS

I DID SOMETHING BAD

Have you ever done a bad thing you're proud of?

Can you think of a time when you knew you did the wrong thing but didn't care?

A time when lying, cheating, or stealing felt justified.

A time when being bad felt so so good.

A time when you lost your moral compass and loved it.

Celebrate your most deliciously bad moment.

Write.

FIRST THOUGHTS

DON'T BLAME ME

How many hearts have you broken?

Look, there's nobody to blame here. The truth is, most people don't deserve your love. You know it, but they don't. You're bound to leave some broken hearts in your wake.

Write about the cracked, mangled, wounded hearts you've created.

Whose heart did you break carefully?

And whose heart were you the most careless with?

Write.

FIRST THOUGHTS

DELICATE

What kind of reputation do you have?

Are you known for anything you wish you weren't known for?

Is there anything about yourself you'd like to delete from other people's brains?

Write about a person who sees you for you, despite your worst qualities. Someone who doesn't care about your reputation.

How has this person treated you delicately?

Write.

FIRST THOUGHTS

LOOK WHAT YOU MADE ME DO

Write a letter to your past self.

Start with the phrase "look what you made me do."

Include:

A mistake you made.

Something you shouldn't have done.

Something you'll never do again.

Write.

FIRST THOUGHTS

SO IT GOES...

Does doing a bad thing make you a bad person?

We all make mistakes.
We're all imperfect.
We all do things we regret.
So it goes.

Make a list of your worst moments.
The things you can't believe you said or did.
So it goes.

Now look at your list.
Pick one bad deed to examine more closely.
Why did you do what you did?
What can you learn from it?
So it goes.

Write.

BONUS: Turn to page 89 of Kurt Vonnegut's *Slaughterhouse-Five* and circle all the adjectives. Do any of these words apply to how you feel about your bad deeds?

FIRST THOUGHTS

GORGEOUS

Who do you ache for?

Gush about your crush.
(This can be a romantic crush, a friend crush, or a talent crush.
Anyone who consumes your thoughts!)

Dissect your emotions for this person.
Get super granular.

What's the most beautiful thing about them?
Why do they make you happy?
What makes them unique?
How do they enrich your life?

Make your yearning for them palpable.

Write.

FIRST THOUGHTS

GETAWAY CAR

Are you more likely to have a difficult conversation or to run away when things get tough?

Make a list of the worst relationship crimes you've committed.

Have you ever ghosted someone?
Lied to them?
Cheated on them?
Stolen from them?

Now choose one of these offenses and analyze your motivations.
How do you feel about it now?
Would you do things differently if you could?

Write.

FIRST THOUGHTS

KING OF MY HEART

Who's the best person you know?

What can you learn about "being good" from this person?

Think about how they interact with the world.
Investigate why you think of them as a good person.
Ask yourself where this goodness comes from.
What do you know about how they became the person they are?

Celebrate this person's many virtues.

Write.

FIRST THOUGHTS

DANCING WITH OUR HANDS TIED

Have you ever loved someone in secret?

Or maybe you loved them more than they loved you, so you held yourself back. Maybe you were afraid of pushing them away.

Whatever the reason, you felt like your hands were tied. You felt like you couldn't be your complete self.

Now imagine you'd been allowed to express yourself fully. How would you have loved this person differently?

Pretend you're shouting your answer across a crowded room and you want everyone to hear about your love.

Write.

FIRST THOUGHTS

DRESS

What do you wear for yourself and what do you wear for other people?

Think about the clothes you own and put them into two different categories:

- Clothes I like to wear.
- Clothes I feel like I should wear.

What do the clothes in each category say about you?
How do the clothes in each category make you feel?
What parts of yourself do the clothes in each category bring out?

Imagine these clothes belong to two different people. Write a conversation between these two people about what they're each trying to say to the world with their style choices.

Write.

FIRST THOUGHTS

THIS IS WHY WE CAN'T HAVE NICE THINGS

Make a list of nice things that make you feel Gatsby.

You're feelin' so Gatsby . . .

. . . when everything comes easy.
. . . when you don't care how much it costs.
. . . when you put on that extra special outfit.
. . . when the music hits just right on the dance floor.
. . . when the sun beams down on you at the beach.

How do those Gatsby moments affect your state of mind?

Do you have enough Gatsby moments in your life?

How could you make your life more Gatsby?

Write.

BONUS: Flip through F. Scott Fitzgerald's *The Great Gatsby* and pick a random phrase to incorporate into your writing.

FIRST THOUGHTS

CALL IT WHAT YOU WANT

If you could make a fresh start...
If you could be someone new...
Who would you want to be?

Think big.
Imagine you can be anyone or anything.
A new you, on your own terms.

You 2.0.

What does this new life look like?
Describe a typical day.
Think of it as a novel and detail the beginning, middle, and ending.
Call it what you want.

Visualize this potential new chapter.
Then ask yourself if there's any way to have pieces of this new life in your current life.
How can you make the fantasy real?

Write.

FIRST THOUGHTS

NEW YEAR'S DAY

Think of a memory you want to hold onto forever.

Why do you cherish this moment so much?

Who else was part of this memory?

Try to envision this memory through someone else's eyes.

Put yourself in their shoes.

How would they tell the story differently?

Which version is closer to reality?

What makes yours better than theirs?

Write.

FIRST THOUGHTS

I FORGOT THAT YOU EXISTED

Do you have any mortal enemies?

Think of someone who did you wrong.
Like, really wrong.

Someone who hurt you badly.
Someone who left an emotional scar.
Someone you spend too much time thinking about.
Someone who doesn't deserve your attention.

It's time to stop giving this person space in your head.

How?
By writing a letter to yourself, explaining how unimportant they are.

Convince yourself to forget about them.

Don't look back.

Write.

FIRST THOUGHTS

CRUEL SUMMER

You said you were fine, but it wasn't true.

We've all told lies about how we're feeling.
Sometimes it's just easier not to get into it.
It's easier to pretend everything's okay than to open up.
Vulnerability can be so freaking scary.
But right now, no one else is listening.
It's just you and this book.
Don't lie to the book.
Open up about all the ways you don't feel fine.
Put your weird, messy, complicated emotions into words.
What are you scared to tell other people?
Don't think about it too much—just pour it out onto the page.
Go. Do it now.

Write.

P.S.
Read what you just wrote.
Would it help to share any of this with a friend?

FIRST THOUGHTS

LOVER

Close your eyes and visualize a moment 20 years from now...30 years from now...40 years from now.

Who do you picture with you in these visions of the future?

Who do you want to tell your future secrets to?
Who do you want to go on future adventures with?
Who do you want to grow old with?

It can be a romantic partner, a friend, a family member—or you can write about someone you haven't met yet.

If "all's well that ends well,"
what will it take for the next 20, 30, 40 years to feel rich and full?

Write.

BONUS: In Shakespeare's play *All's Well That Ends Well*, the Countess says, "Love all, trust a few, Do wrong to none." Who do you trust with all your heart? Include them in your vision of the future.

FIRST THOUGHTS

THE MAN

If you weren't worried about what other people thought of you, what would you do to get ahead?

Make a list of all the things that stop you from being the person you want to be.

What keeps you from getting everything you want? From doing everything you want to do?

If you had more power, how would things be different?

If nothing held you back, what would success look like?

Brainstorm ten things you could do to feel—and BE—more powerful.

Write.

FIRST THOUGHTS

THE ARCHER

Would you rather be the pursuer or the pursued?

Think of a time when you pursued a relationship. A job. An experience.

Are you a good hunter? Are you persistent? Are you clever? Are you good at coming up with different tactics to get what you want?

Now think of a time when someone else pursued you, or an opportunity was presented to you. Did you play hard to get? How did it feel to know you were wanted?

Which of these roles, pursuer or pursued, felt the most natural to you? What do you think this says about who you are?

Write.

FIRST THOUGHTS

I THINK HE KNOWS

Think of someone you love.

Do they know you love them?
What three things do you love most about them?

Do they know what you admire about them?
What three things do you admire most about them?

Do they know how much they've taught you?
What three lessons have you learned from them?

Do they know what you would miss about them if they were gone?
What three things would you miss most?

Do they know your most cherished memories of them?
What are the best moments you've shared?

Write.

FIRST THOUGHTS

MISS AMERICANA &
THE HEARTBREAK PRINCE

What are you Most Likely To . . . ?

You know the Senior Superlative awards they give out in high school yearbooks? Best Hair. Best Dressed. Most Likely to Be a Star. Life of the Party. Most Athletic. And so on.

What if you could win superlatives in your everyday life? What superlative would you win and why?

Most Likely to Arrive Late to Brunch.
Best Gift Giver.
Least Likely to Answer a Text Message Promptly.
Best Drunk Karaoke Singer.

You can pick anything—let your imagination run wild.

Write.

FIRST THOUGHTS

PAPER RINGS

What have you been waiting your whole life for?

When we're young, we have so many ideas about how our lives might turn out. We anticipate a life well-lived. We imagine the person we'll be when we're old, all the experiences we'll have, the hopes that will come to fruition.

But we don't know what twists and turns await us.

Whatever age you are, one thing is true for everyone:
There is a dream you thought would have come true by now. A dream you still wish would happen.

Write about this dream.
Why do you want it?
How will it affect you if you never quite get it?
Can you find meaning in this dream's absence?

Write.

FIRST THOUGHTS

CORNELIA STREET

How are your memories shaped by where they took place?

How many streets have you lived on?

Write the name of each street at the top of separate pieces of paper.

Look at the first street and brainstorm the most significant things that happened to you on this street. The memories, good and bad. The times when your life shifted in some way.

Think of significant moments you associate with each street.

If each street represents a different chapter in your life, what would you name each chapter?

If you've only ever lived on one or two streets, can you identify chapters within your time living in these places?

What images, emotions, sensations, memories do the streets from your past evoke?

Write.

FIRST THOUGHTS

DEATH BY A THOUSAND CUTS

Make a list of the significant "goodbyes" you've lived through. Come up with as many as you can.

Homes you've moved out of.

Cities you've left behind.

Friends you've outgrown.

Loved ones who aren't with us anymore.

Breakups that still hurt.

How have these various goodbyes shaped you?

Write.

FIRST THOUGHTS

LONDON BOY

Where does your heart live?

Is there a place that means so much to you it aches?
A place you see when you close your eyes?
A place you wish you could be right now?

Write about why you long for this location.
What does it mean to you?

It might be a place you've spent a lot of time in, or a place you've only been to once. It might even be a place you feel connected to but have never seen.

Explore all the reasons you love this place so deeply.

Write.

FIRST THOUGHTS

SOON YOU'LL GET BETTER

Write a benediction for a loved one who's ill.

No one wants to spend time in a hospital waiting room, but it's inevitable. Difficult moments waiting to get news of a loved one's health or prognosis. Desperate moments. Holding onto hope.

Think of a loved one who needs good health news.
Write the words "soon you'll get better because" and then finish that statement with as many hopeful sentiments as you can.

How many reasons can you think of for them to get out of the hospital and get on with their life?

Write.

FIRST THOUGHTS

FALSE GOD

What are you absolutely obsessed with?

Where did this obsession begin?
Can you remember when the very first seed of interest was planted and how it grew?
Get to the root of it.

Explore how your obsession makes you feel.
Be so earnest it's embarrassing.
This is your moment to obsess about what it's like to have this obsession.

Now think about how you could recruit a companion to share your passion for this thing. How could you spark this obsession in someone else?

Write.

FIRST THOUGHTS

YOU NEED TO CALM DOWN

Do you have any haters?

Tell them to calm down.
Do it politely.
Do it rudely.
Do it with grace.
Do it with the rage of a thousand wild boars.
Do it like they're five-years-old.
Do it like they're a complete idiot.

Tell them to get help.

Tell them how their hatred makes you feel.

Tell them how their words hurt you.

Tell them about the ramifications of their actions.

Tell them to shut up.

Tell them why they need therapy.

Tell them to calm down.

Write.

FIRST THOUGHTS

AFTERGLOW

Have you ever broken something you loved?

This can be a literal object or a metaphorical one.

If you did it on purpose . . . why?
What were you afraid of?
What did you hope to achieve?
Did it work?

If you did it because of carelessness . . . were you able to fix things later?

Did this broken love change you in any way?

Write.

FIRST THOUGHTS

ME!

What's the most unique thing about you?

Imagine you've just been rejected.
The person who rejected you shows up at your door.
They ask for another chance.

Give them ten reasons why they don't deserve you.

What's the most fascinating thing about you?
Explain why there's no one else like you.
Make them regret how they treated you.
Make them see what a catch you are.
Show them your light.

Write.

FIRST THOUGHTS

IT'S NICE TO HAVE A FRIEND

When was the last time you told your best friend how much they mean to you?

What makes your best friend different from your other friends?

What would they understand more than anyone else?

Do you have any inside jokes?

How do you complement each other?

Imagine how terrible the world would be without them. Make a list of things you would miss about them if they weren't here.

Write.

FIRST THOUGHTS

DAYLIGHT

Write about a new beginning.

An unexpected new chapter.
A big life change.
A pivot.
A time when you emerged from a personal cocoon.
A transformation.
A shift from night into day.

How would you define this new era you entered?
Look at how this new you interacts with the world and celebrate
how much you've grown.

Write.

FIRST THOUGHTS

THE 1

Write about a no that you're ready to say yes to.

It's time to embrace some new shit.

Take a look at all the big decisions you've ever made, specifically any opportunities you've turned down.

Have you changed your mind about any of your choices?

Draw an emotional line from the moment when you said no to the moment you realized you felt differently.

Try to make sense of the journey you've been on.

What can you do to get a second chance?

Write.

FIRST THOUGHTS

CARDIGAN

Write about something you figured out about life when you were very young.

Life is full of lessons—wonderful lessons, hard lessons, confusing lessons.

Write about something you knew before anyone else knew you knew it. Something that belonged to you and only you.

How did it feel to contain hidden depths?

Write.

FIRST THOUGHTS

THE LAST GREAT AMERICAN DYNASTY

Write about a historical figure you feel drawn to.

What qualities of theirs do you most admire?

In what ways do you aspire to be more like them?

Quickly jot down ten reasons you think they've impacted history.

Imagine a conversation with this person. What would you ask them? How do you think they might answer?

Write.

FIRST THOUGHTS

EXILE

Write about a red flag you noticed too late.

It was always there.

If you'd been a little more careful, maybe you could have seen the ending at the beginning.

Write about that red flag you didn't want to see.
That warning sign you should have heeded.

What was your blind spot?

Write.

FIRST THOUGHTS

MY TEARS RICOCHET

Write about a messy ending or goodbye.

Do you believe in ghosts? What about ghosts of past failed relationships? Are you haunted by things you said to an ex?

Sure, it would be great if we could always end things gracefully, but hey, we're human.

Take a journey back to the last gasps of a past relationship. Don't push away the details you wish you could forget. Write about those bad moments.

Now write about the last good moment you had with that person.

When did you realize the bad outweighed the good?

What took you so long?

Write.

FIRST THOUGHTS

MIRRORBALL

How many versions of yourself exist within you?

Everyone puts on different masks for different people. You behave one way with your best friend and another way with your lover and another way with your weird aunt and another way with that cute barista and another way with your parents, and on and on and on. Sometimes it's hard to keep every version of yourself straight!

Have you ever shown anyone every side of yourself?

How would it feel to be seen by someone who wants to know you completely? Even the parts you're not proud of.

Do you know that kind of vulnerability?

Could you ever let down all your walls?

Write.

FIRST THOUGHTS

SEVEN

What's your best summer memory?

When did it take place?
Where were you?
Describe the sights, smells, and sounds you associate with this memory.
What songs remind you of this time in your life?
Do you remember what you were wearing?

Quickly jot down five words you associate with this memory.
Five evocative words.
Actually, no—jot down two more words now. Seven words total!

If you could relive this perfect summer day, would you do it exactly the same? Or is there something you would change?

Can you plan to make a similar memory next summer?

What would you have to do to make that happen?

Write.

FIRST THOUGHTS

AUGUST

What are you hopeful about?

Sometimes I get superstitious. I worry that if I express something I want—if I say it out loud—then it won't ever happen. It's like I'm afraid that the universe, or some higher power, will hear about my desire and laugh because now they know how to thwart me. It's a dumb superstition, but it makes me keep my hopes inside. Do you do this too?

The problem is, I also believe that when we're really clear about the things we want—the things we're hoping for—then we're more likely to work to make them happen. If you don't know what you want, then how are you supposed to get what you want? You know?

Write down a hope that you're afraid to vocalize.
Clarify it for yourself.
Make your hope feel more real.

Write.

FIRST THOUGHTS

THIS IS ME TRYING

What are you having a hard time adjusting to right now?

Do you hate change?
Here's the thing—we're always changing. And everything around us is in a constant state of change. It's just the big, sudden changes that feel jarring. Those are the changes we fight against. But the little changes? Most of them we don't even think about.

Write about a change you're struggling to wrap your head around.

Write about a change you really want to be okay with.

What will it take to make things feel okay?

Write.

FIRST THOUGHTS

ILLICIT AFFAIRS

How far would you go to keep a secret?

Are you good at keeping other people's secrets?

Are you good at keeping your own?

What's the most illicit thing you've secretly done?

Think about why you did it.

Think about how you felt afterwards.

Would you ever do it again?

Write.

BONUS: Read Robert Frost's poem "The Road Not Taken." Find the 13th word in the poem. Do you have any secret desires, hopes, or dreams related to this activity?

FIRST THOUGHTS

INVISIBLE STRING

Do you believe in destiny?

You know that feeling when something clicks into place, and you sense that you're exactly where you're supposed to be?

When was the last time you had that "everything is just right" feeling?

Describe this encounter with destiny.

Write.

FIRST THOUGHTS

MAD WOMAN

What makes you furious?

Write about your anger
and as you write about it
let it build
and grow
and take on a life of its own.

Clarify exactly WHY you're angry.

Then make a list of ten things you can do about it.
Ten actions you can take.
How can you make your anger productive?
How can you use your madness?
Can you create anything with it?

Write.

FIRST THOUGHTS

EPIPHANY

Have you ever witnessed something so ugly you wish you could flush it from your memory?

An act of hatred.
Humanity at its worst.
A moment of pure ugliness.
An act of war, either metaphoric or literal.

The kind of thing you just can't make any sense of.

Try to make sense of it now.

Write.

FIRST THOUGHTS

BETTY

Write an overdue apology.

Think of someone you've treated badly.
Close your eyes and imagine yourself in their shoes.
Imagine how your behavior affected them.
Try to feel their pain.

Now write this person a letter.
Begin with the words, "I'm sorry I hurt you."
Do not use the word "if."

Be specific about why you're sorry.
Take accountability for your actions.
Don't make any excuses.
Just reflect on who you were at the time and what you did and
how you see, now, that you behaved badly.

Write.

FIRST THOUGHTS

PEACE

What if you stopped trying to be perfect?

When we try to be perfect, we set ourselves up for failure.

Instead of "perfect," what if we just did our best?

What does your best look like right now.
Not yesterday, not tomorrow.
Today.
Now.

What kind of friend can you be?
What kind of lover?
What kind of partner?

What's the best you can do?
The best you can be?
Would it be enough?

Write.

FIRST THOUGHTS

HOAX

Have you left part of yourself in another city?

The other day I was watching a movie that was shot in a place I love, I place I haven't been to in years, and it was hard to focus on the film. I felt such an ache. Do you have a place like that?

Why do you feel so connected to this place?
What was your first impression of this place?
How have your feelings for this place evolved over time?

Come up with an itinerary for the next time you go there.

Write.

FIRST THOUGHTS

THE LAKES

Imagine you lived in a world without social media.

How do you know you're having a good time if no one's out there to see your post and maybe even share it?

Think about how much time you spend on your phone, either scrolling or posting. Then, suddenly, poof, all those distractions are gone. Take a moment to really imagine how that would change your life.

What would you do differently?
How would you live differently?
What would you want?
What would you desire?
Who would you want to be with?
What would you make?
How would you express yourself?

Write.

BONUS: Read William Wordsworth's poem "I Wandered Lonely as a Cloud." Examine the various ways your "heart with pleasure [might] fill" in this alternate world without social media.

FIRST THOUGHTS

WILLOW

Are there any stories in your life that have taken on the power of myth?

There are some stories that grow the more we tell them. Stories that gain significance over the years.

Stories that evolve until you don't even know how much they resemble the truth anymore.

We all have stories that have become larger than life.

What is your most mythical story?

Write.

FIRST THOUGHTS

CHAMPAGNE PROBLEMS

What are your most insignificant problems?

Look, they might be insignificant, but they still weigh on you. So go ahead and complain.

It's okay.

Whatever you're holding tightly inside your chest, acknowledge it. Maybe writing about these dumb, little, seemingly mundane problems will help you move past them.

So express yourself.

How do these stupid problems affect your life?

Write.

FIRST THOUGHTS

GOLD RUSH

What stories make up the personal folklore of your family?

I'm talking about the stories your family tells over and over and over again.

As you think through these stories, ask yourself: which one says the most about your family?

Which one would you choose to put into a time capsule for future generations of your family to read?

Tell that story now. Include all the juicy details.

Write.

FIRST THOUGHTS

'TIS THE DAMN SEASON

Write about something you've had a difficult time giving up.

Maybe it's a bad habit . . .

Maybe it's a toxic relationship . . .

Whatever it is, you KNOW it's not good for you.

So why is it so hard to quit this habit?

Why is it so hard to say goodbye to this person?

Why do you let them linger? What are you holding onto?

Write.

FIRST THOUGHTS

TOLERATE IT

No one wants to be "tolerated." What a horrible feeling.

We want to be seen. We want to be celebrated. We want to be loved.

But there will always be people who undervalue us. Who don't appreciate what we have to offer.

Think of someone who doesn't treat you the way you deserve to be treated. (This could be someone from your past or someone from your present.)

What would happen if you confronted them?

What would happen if you told them exactly how they make you feel?

Imagine how that conversation might go.

Write.

FIRST THOUGHTS

NO BODY, NO CRIME

Have you ever been the subject of gossip?

What's the worst thing anyone ever said about you?

Call them out.

Turn this "gossip" into a strength.

Reclaim the story.

Write.

FIRST THOUGHTS

HAPPINESS

Pick a moment in the future.

It could be 5 years from now, 10 years, 20 years.

Imagine who you might be then.

What do you want future you to know?

What do you want future you to love?

What do you want future you to look like?

What do you want future you to feel like?

Make a list of things you want future you to have accomplished.

What makes future you happy?

Write.

FIRST THOUGHTS

DOROTHEA

Does it ever startle you when you see a friend on social media and realize how long it's been since you've seen them in real life?

Write a letter to a friend you haven't talked to in years.

Connect with them now.

Tell them something you love about them.

Tell them something you miss about them.

And then tell them three things you hope for them.

Write.

FIRST THOUGHTS

CONEY ISLAND

What are you too old for?

Make a list of activities and behavior you're ready to leave in the past.

Look at your list and circle whatever has the most energy around it.

Think about the person who used to do that thing that you circled.

How is that person different from the person you are today?

Write.

FIRST THOUGHTS

IVY

What's your relationship with nature?

Think of a beach, or a forest, or a desert. Whatever image you land on, close your eyes and imagine yourself in this place. Picture it in as much detail as you can. Is it high or low tide? What trees are you surrounded by? What does that rock underneath your toes feel like?

Now imagine someone's with you. Someone you love.

How and why do they fit in this specific landscape? Explore all the ways this person is like a beach, or a forest, or a desert.

Paint a portrait of them using these images from nature.

Write.

BONUS: Look at the fourth line of the poem "Compassion" by Miller Williams. Have you ever heard "things no ears have heard" or seen things "no eyes have seen"? Incorporate these memories into your writing.

FIRST THOUGHTS

COWBOY LIKE ME

Have you ever pretended to be someone you aren't to get ahead?

You know the advice to fake it 'til you make it? It's like an act of make-believe. When I do it, it makes me feel like a con artist. On the inside I'm screaming *please don't realize I'm not as confident about this as I'm trying to convince you I am*!

Write about a time when you faked it.
Did the con work?
Did you eventually make it?

Write.

FIRST THOUGHTS

LONG STORY SHORT

How did you get where you are?

If I asked you to give me the "long story short" version of your life story—just the big headlines—what moments would you focus on?

What was your beginning?

What are the highlights since then?

What was your most interesting detour?

And where are you going next?

Write.

FIRST THOUGHTS

MARJORIE

Who do you wish you could talk to one more time?

Imagine they're here right now.

Quickly jot down some of your favorite things about them, to help make them feel more present.

Now imagine you could ask them for advice.
What do you want them to say to you?
Channel their energy.

Write.

FIRST THOUGHTS

CLOSURE

Write about an unsatisfying ending.

We don't always get the closure we need. Some endings are messy. They're incomplete. They're unsatisfying. Sometimes you don't even realize you experienced an ending until long after the fact. You didn't get to take it in. You didn't get to process it.

Put it to rest now.
Say what you need to say.
Feel it.
Give it proper attention.
Look at it clearly.
Then close that door.

Write.

FIRST THOUGHTS

EVERMORE

You know how a bad moment feels like it'll last forever? Then when you make it to the other side, you remember bad moments always pass?

Think about a bad moment—a loss, a sadness, or a trial that you survived.

Remember how it felt in the moment.

Write a letter to your future self.
For your next bad moment.
Or loss.
Or sadness.
Or trial.
Remind yourself how you got through it before.
Tell yourself that this won't go on forevermore.

Describe the light on the other side.

Write.

FIRST THOUGHTS

RIGHT WHERE YOU LEFT ME

Is there anything you've been told you're supposed to want that you just don't?

When we're growing up, we take in so many lessons about what our lives are supposed to look like.

But what if you don't want marriage? What if your views on love aren't as traditional as you were taught they should be?

What if you don't want kids? What if you love the freedom your life without kids affords you?

What if you don't want a house with a mortgage and all the upkeep it requires?

Who decided our ultimate goals in life should be marriage, kids, and home ownership?

Why?

Explore how you deviate from "the norm" and why you like it.

Write.

FIRST THOUGHTS

IT'S TIME TO GO

Write about a bittersweet farewell.

What did you learn from your most complicated goodbye?

Even though you knew it was time to go, that doesn't mean it was easy to do.

So how did you get through it?

Or are you still in the process of moving on?

Write.

FIRST THOUGHTS

LAVENDER HAZE

Write about an obsession that consumes you.

Is there anything for which you have so much love that when you're thinking about it you can't think about anything else? Like the outer edges of your consciousness get all hazy, and this is all you can see?

How did this obsession start?

How does this obsession fuel you?

Where would you be without this obsession?

Why does this obsession give you so much joy?

Write.

FIRST THOUGHTS

MAROON

A hundred years from now, if someone was reading about your life, what would you want them to learn about you?

After we're gone, we're all going to leave some sort of legacy behind. So . . .

What do you want your legacy to be?

Imagine your boldest, most wonderful future.

Imagine you're writing a journal entry specifically meant for a future biographer. What important chapters do you want to make sure they cover? (Include chapters from your life you've already lived and make up future chapters you hope to make into a reality.)

Write.

FIRST THOUGHTS

ANTI-HERO

It's you, hi, you're the problem, it's you.

What are your most problematic qualities?
What areas of your life need the most improvement?
What valuable life lessons have you never learned?

Do you lack courage?
Have you ever made a mistake on purpose?
When was the last time you lied, cheated, or stole?
What parts of your life feel morally gray?

How do these imperfections make you more real?

Write.

FIRST THOUGHTS

SNOW ON THE BEACH

Write about something in your life that's weird but beautiful at the same time.

Something that feels wrong but right.

Something that shouldn't be. But is.

Something that feels incredible because you know how unique it is.

Something that makes you believe in magic.

Is there anything in your life that fills you with wonder? THAT'S what I want you to write about.

Write.

FIRST THOUGHTS

YOU'RE ON YOUR OWN, KID

Give yourself a pep talk.

Is there anything you need to do that you've been putting off because it's scary?

Pull off the emotional bandaid.

Talk yourself into it.

Tell yourself you can do it.

Talk yourself through how it's going to go.

Practice it.

Do it now.

Imagine a few different ways it might go.

Be brave.

Write.

FIRST THOUGHTS

MIDNIGHT RAIN

What's the biggest transformation you've ever gone through?

Think of yourself before, then think of yourself after.

If the "before" you could ask the "after" you a question, what would they ask?

Actually, why stop at one question? Make a list of as many questions from your earlier self as possible.

When you're done coming up with questions . . . answer them.

Write.

FIRST THOUGHTS

QUESTION...?

How do you feel about public displays of affection?

Are you comfortable with PDA?

Or are you the type of person who yells "get a room" at strangers?

Or maybe you're somewhere in between . . .

Wherever you land on the PDA spectrum, what do you think this says about you?

Write.

FIRST THOUGHTS

VIGILANTE SHIT

Who have you been wronged by?

Write about how their actions made you feel. Write about how they hurt you. Let yourself feel the anger and sadness. Then delete it. Erase it. Rip up the pages those words were written on. Burn it if you can. Let yourself feel those intense feelings, then strip them of their power.

When the smoke clears, write about all the ways you're better than this other person.

Now that you've made it clear they didn't get the best of you, move on. Write about what that looks like—especially how the future is going to be so much better than the time you spent with the person who wronged you.

Write.

FIRST THOUGHTS

BEJEWELED

Do you ever feel like you shimmer?

How and when and where are you at your best?

Imagine a sociologist is studying these moments. Or maybe a photographer is preparing to capture your essence.

What would they say?
How would they describe your aura?
How would they analyze your charm?
How would they capture your beauty?

Write.

FIRST THOUGHTS

LABYRINTH

Let's take a moment to look at our emotional wounds that haven't quite healed.

Maybe it's too painful or scary to face these wounds head on.

That's okay. Even if you don't bounce back quickly, that doesn't mean you'll never bounce back.

So turn the wound around and around and look at it from every angle.

Think about what you get from the pain.
Is there a part of you that needs it?

Examine who you were before you had this pain and how this pain has changed you. Imagine how your life will be better when you can let it go.

Write.

FIRST THOUGHTS

KARMA

Do you believe in karma?

When has karma helped you?
When has karma hurt you?

How does karma affect the way you behave on a daily basis?

Do you do good deeds because they're rewarding?
Or do you do good deeds because you don't want the universe to punish you?

Brainstorm at least two good deeds you could do today.
Brainstorm at least five good deeds you could do this week.
Brainstorm at least three bigger good deeds you could do this year.

Write.

FIRST THOUGHTS

SWEET NOTHING

What "small kindnesses" have other people shown you that you'll never forget?

Make a list of these acts of kindness.

Then look at your list and circle the kindness that speaks to you most deeply.

Why does this act of kindness resonate with you so much?

Who committed this act of kindness? What does it say about them? What can you learn from them?

Write.

FIRST THOUGHTS

MASTERMIND

Are you a sneaky person?

What's the most duplicitous thing you've ever done?

If you're really digging deep, then this is probably something you'd be too embarrassed to admit to anyone else.

It's okay—you don't have to tell anyone else right now.

But confess your deviousness to yourself.

Don't hold back anything.

Write.

FIRST THOUGHTS

HITS DIFFERENT

Are you good at listening to your gut?

Write about a time when you wanted something to be right, but you instinctively knew it was wrong.

What were the warning signs?

Did it take you time to see them?

Now write about a time when you immediately knew something was right.

How did it hit differently?

Write.

FIRST THOUGHTS

THE GREAT WAR

Do you have any past traumas you haven't reckoned with?

Be honest with yourself: is there anything you've avoided dealing with that might be affecting your current relationships?

Why are you afraid to face it?

Let's do a quick exercise. Think of all the times you've done something you were afraid of and then felt better afterwards. What if writing about this trauma could take the power out of it? You don't have to show it to anyone. Just put into words what happened and explore how it makes you feel.

Write.

FIRST THOUGHTS

BIGGER THAN THE WHOLE SKY

Think of someone you put on a pedestal.

Maybe it's a romantic partner, or a parent, or a teacher, or even a celebrity crush.

How many similes can you come up with to describe this person's greatness? What comparisons can you make that describe this person best?

What is this person bigger than?

What is this person brighter than?

What is this person bolder than?

And so on.

Write.

FIRST THOUGHTS

PARIS

Have you ever created a false reality?

When we're kids, we play make-believe all the time. Who says we can't incorporate that into our daily lives as adults?

Have you ever faked an emotion?
Have you ever pretended to be someone you aren't?
How active is your imagination?

Let it run wild as you explore your personal history of make-believe.

Write.

FIRST THOUGHTS

HIGH INFIDELITY

How many personal storms have you endured?

Think of yourself as a city.

Now think of the dramatic events of your life as acts of weather.

When was your last bit of rain?
What's the worst hurricane you've been through?
How many earthquakes have you survived?
Have you ever experienced a monsoon?

What can you do to protect your city from the next natural disaster?

Write.

FIRST THOUGHTS

GLITCH

What's the most unexpected thing that's ever happened to you?

Have you ever had a moment that felt too good to be true? Has your life ever taken such a huge, radical turn that it almost didn't feel real?

Write about a time when your life pivoted in such a surreal way that it felt like it must have been some sort of glitch.

Look at how you thought things would go, then look at how they actually went, and write about the chasm in between.

Why was it such a surprise?

Write.

FIRST THOUGHTS

WOULD'VE, SHOULD'VE, COULD'VE

Write an apology to yourself.

Think of a mistake you made in the past.

If you knew then what you know now, what would you have done differently? How should you have handled things better? What could you have done to change the outcome of events?

Choose a mistake that still haunts you.

Write.

FIRST THOUGHTS

DEAR READER

Dear writer, what's the worst advice anyone ever gave you?

Dear writer, how did you figure out this advice was terrible?

Dear writer, how would you rewrite this advice?

Dear writer, what's the best advice you've ever been given?

Did you take it?

Dear writer, what's the best advice you've ever given someone else?

Did they take it?

Write.

FIRST THOUGHTS

FORTNIGHT

What's the unhealthiest love you've ever felt?

Write about a love you've grown to hate.
A love that burned bright, then extinguished fast.
A love that feels like treason now.
A love you're glad to be done with.

Write about how this love tricked you.
Write about the damage this love did.
Write about how you got out.

How can you ensure that you'll never get tricked again?

Write.

FIRST THOUGHTS

THE TORTURED POETS DEPARTMENT

Write an ode to an activity that's become outdated or forgotten.

Who uses typewriters anymore?
Who writes love letters by hand?
Who sends letters to loved ones in the mail?
Who leaves long rambling voicemails for their friends?
Who writes in cursive?
Who owns a dictionary and looks up words they don't know?
Who writes notes in the margins of their favorite book?
Who writes poetry on random scraps of paper when they don't have anything else to write on?

If you answered "me" to any of these questions, write about it. What other outdated or forgotten talents do you possess?

Write.

BONUS: Have you ever listened to Patti Smith's album *Horses*? It's only 43 minutes long. Put away your phone and any other technology invented after 1975 and listen to *Horses* in its entirety right now. Taylor would approve. It could change your life.

FIRST THOUGHTS

MY BOY ONLY BREAKS HIS FAVORITE TOYS

What excuses have you made for someone who should treat you better?

He loves me, though.
She doesn't really mean it.
They're going through a tough time right now.
He won't do it again.
She promised to change.
They didn't know it upset me.

Write about a broken relationship.
One you're in right now, or one from your past.

What should you have known sooner?
How do you know when it's time to move on?

Write.

FIRST THOUGHTS

DOWN BAD

Write about a wild attraction.

Do you have any attractions you're ashamed to admit to? You know your friends, or your family, won't get it, so you keep this attraction to yourself.

But you feel A PULL.
It feels COSMIC, almost.
Out of your control.

Write about this desire.
Unpack it.
Figure out where it comes from.
What makes you so down bad?

Write.

FIRST THOUGHTS

SO LONG, LONDON

How much sad do you have in you?

Look at something that makes you feel sorrow.
A pain in your heart.
An unbearable heaviness.

Tell this pain to go away.
Tell it you've moved on.
Even if you don't feel like you've moved on, fake it for this exercise.

Have a conversation with these difficult feelings and tell them you're done with tragedy. Tell them you're moving your life into a different genre.

Write.

FIRST THOUGHTS

BUT DADDY I LOVE HIM

Do you feel like a grown up? Or are there still parts of you that suffer from arrested development?

Write about this duality: the juxtaposition of what you know vs. what you still haven't learned.

What's the youngest thing about you?
What's the oldest thing about you?

What do you still want to learn?
What do you wish you didn't know?

Look at your gray areas.

How can you grow the parts you left behind?

Write.

FIRST THOUGHTS

FRESH OUT THE SLAMMER

Imagine you've been sent to jail for a year. You're not allowed contact with anyone while you're inside. Who would be your first phone call the day you get out?

Go with the first person who popped into your head.
Don't overthink it.
Even if they don't feel like the right answer, maybe your subconscious is trying to tell you something, so just embrace it.

Why is this person so important to you?
What's the first question you'd ask them?
What's the first thing you'd want to tell them?
What would you want to know about what you missed?

Explore all the reasons you feel so deeply connected to this person.

Write.

FIRST THOUGHTS

FLORIDA!!!

How many ghosts do you know?

A ghost could be a person from your past you don't see anymore. Someone who haunts you.

A ghost could be a place from your past you haven't been to in a while. A place you miss deeply.

A ghost could be a person, place, or thing that doesn't exist anymore. You feel their absence in the place they once were.

Catalogue the ghosts who haunt you.
Why do you think they cling to you so desperately?

Write.

FIRST THOUGHTS

GUILTY AS SIN?

Have you ever stolen something?

Did you get away with it?
How and why did you do it?

Think about the person you stole from.
What did your stolen item mean to them?
What was the impact of your theft?

Think beyond the possible monetary value. What emotional ripples did your theft incur?

Write.

FIRST THOUGHTS

WHO'S AFRAID OF
LITTLE OLD ME?

Have you ever been plagued by a rumor?

It doesn't matter if the rumor was true or not—what we're looking at here is how the rumor affected you.

How did it feel to know people were talking about you?
How did you react?

How did you contain the scandal?

Come up with at least five metaphors to describe how it felt to have other people obsessing over your personal business.

Now that you have some distance from the rumor, what would you like to say to the people who spread it?

Write.

FIRST THOUGHTS

I CAN FIX HIM (NO REALLY I CAN)

Have you ever tried to fix someone?

Okay, let's get this out of the way first: you can't make someone change. If they're going to change, they have to want to change first. And you can't force it.

But what if you could?
Would you?

Whoa!
Hold on.
Why do you want to "fix" them?

What does it even mean to fix a person?

How would you feel if someone tried to fix you?

Write.

FIRST THOUGHTS

LOML

There is someone living rent free in your head right now. It's time to give them an eviction notice.

Think of someone who used to take up a lot of your time.
Someone you got used to managing.
Someone you've said goodbye to, but still have complicated feelings for. Or maybe you never got closure with them—things ended in a messy way so it's been hard to move on.

Write about one thing you learned from them.
Write about one thing you want to forget about them.
Write about one reason they were necessary.
Write about one reason they were unnecessary.

Write them out of your story. Shift them into past tense.

Write.

FIRST THOUGHTS

I CAN DO IT WITH A BROKEN HEART

Write about a sorrow you keep hidden.

Show us a glimpse of something inside you that feels broken.
Let us feel your misery.
Let us feel your sadness.

Write about this hurt you've been holding onto, then show what you've written to someone you trust.

Explore how it feels when you're miserable and nobody else knows about it.

Then explore what changes within you when you feel seen.

Write.

FIRST THOUGHTS

THE SMALLEST MAN WHO EVER LIVED

Who's the worst person you've ever met?

Think of someone who treated you terribly.
What lessons do they need to learn?

Do some brainstorming about your own personal value system.
What does being a decent person mean to you?
Feel free to be obvious.
This is stuff they should have learned as a kid!
But clearly they need to learn it now.

They need to be more like you.
What would it take for them to become a better human?

Write.

FIRST THOUGHTS

THE ALCHEMY

It's time to think about transformation.

Specifically, a transformation that occurs when you meet someone special. You know how that magic feels. It can be hard to describe, but some people just wake something up inside you and you feel different after you encounter them.

Write about a person in your life who has changed you.

The combination of who they were and who you were created a little bit of magic, an alchemy, that turned you both into different people.

Can you put it into words?

Write.

FIRST THOUGHTS

CLARA BOW

What public figure do you look up to the most?

Think of someone you idolize.
Don't pick someone you know personally—pick someone whose presence is larger than life.
Someone who's made a great impact on your life.

What have you learned from this person?
How did they change your world view?

If you could meet this person and tell them how much they mean to you, what would you say?

Write.

FIRST THOUGHTS

THE BLACK DOG

Think of someone from your past who has cut you out of their life.

What do you hope they miss about you?
What good thing do you hope they remember about you?
What do you think they got wrong about you?

What do you miss about them?
What good thing do you remember about them?
What do you think you misunderstood about them?

Try to find a sense of peace with their absence.

Write.

FIRST THOUGHTS

IMGONNAGETYOUBACK

Are you a vengeful person?

Do you hold a grudge?
Are you passive-aggressive?
When someone betrays you, do you forgive easily? Or do you let your feelings fester?

Have you ever tried to get back at someone who wronged you?

If you could curse someone from your past—someone who hurt you badly—what pain would you wish upon them? Don't overthink it—express your rage as quickly as possible. Then go back and look over what you've written. Did it help? Do you feel a sense of release? Do you still feel the need to get back at them? Can you write yourself into a place of peace? Try. Keep cursing them until you don't need to anymore.

Write.

FIRST THOUGHTS

THE ALBATROSS

ALBATROSS, noun: an encumbrance; something that makes it impossible for you to live a normal life.

Write about the bad seed in your life.
It could be a person. It could be a job. It could be an addiction. It could be anything, really—but it's something that's getting in the way of your happiness.

How was this seed originally planted?
What have you done to make it grow?
How much damage has this seed done to your garden? Or, to put it plainly, how is this bad seed destroying your life?

Break it all down.
Look at it plainly.

Imagine how your life might improve without this albatross.
How can you make that life a reality?

Write.

BONUS: Taylor references Shakespeare's *Romeo and Juliet* when she sings "A rose by any other name is a scandal." Which is her way of saying this seed is bad no matter how you look at it. But what if she's wrong? Is there any way you could salvage this bad seed? Explore the possibilities in your writing.

FIRST THOUGHTS

CHLOE OR SAM OR SOPHIA OR MARCUS

Write down the words "I loved you the way you were."

Now pick a moment in your past. Any moment.
Yesterday.
Three years ago.
Twenty years ago.
It doesn't matter when—just pick a specific moment you remember well.

Who were you in that moment?
What did you love about that version of yourself?
What do you miss about that version of yourself?

Write.

FIRST THOUGHTS

HOW DID IT END?

Have you ever looked back at a failed relationship and realized you have no idea why it didn't work out? Everything seemed to be going right...until it wasn't.

It's time to conduct a postmortem.
It's time to figure out the true reason why this relationship ended.

You can pick any relationship that's over. A romance gone sour. A best friend who wasn't forever. A family member you've inexplicably become estranged from. They're all fair game.

Try to take the emotion out of it.

Think of yourself as an archeologist on a dig, looking for fossils that might help explain what you once had.

Think of yourself as a sociologist determined to understand human behavior.

Think of yourself as a detective. You have plenty of questions. Find some answers.

Write.

FIRST THOUGHTS

SO HIGH SCHOOL

Write about the first time you saw someone you love.

There are two different people in you.
There's who you were before you saw them for the first time.
And there's the person you were afterwards.

What was your first impression?
What did you get wrong about them?
What did you get right?

Tell them.
Tell them about the first time you saw them.

Explore your first conversation.
Explore the first time you hung out together.
Explore the moment you realized they belonged in your life.
Explore a time they made you laugh.
Really get into what makes them special.
Let your emotions overflow.

Write.

BONUS: What book do you associate with this person? Why?

FIRST THOUGHTS

I HATE IT HERE

What decade do you wish you lived in instead of this one?

What draws you to this other time?
Do you think this era would be good to you?
What would you hate about living there?

Write a vision of yourself in this other time.
Imagine how this other time sounds.
How would you dress in this other time?
How would you behave in this other time?
How would this other time change you?
How does this other time make you feel?

Write.

BONUS: In *The Secret Garden*, Frances Hodgson Burnett writes, "She made herself stronger by fighting with the wind." While you explore life in another decade, ask yourself how you might make yourself stronger by fighting against the cultural mores of that time.

FIRST THOUGHTS

THANK YOU AIMEE

What is your pettiest fantasy?

Think of someone who hurt or betrayed you.
Imagine you're a splinter in their skin.

If you could wish mild emotional turmoil on them, what would it look like?

Don't wish them ill will—you're better than that. No, wish them slight discomfort:

- An awkward encounter with an ex.
- A flat tire when they're already late.
- An upset stomach.

What bitter pills do you hope they swallow?

Write.

FIRST THOUGHTS

I LOOK IN PEOPLE'S WINDOWS

Imagine someone else is looking in your metaphorical windows and wishing they had your life.

Or, in other words, what do you think strangers might envy about the way you live?

What do you take for granted?

What blessings have you forgotten to count?

Look at your own life from the outside and take stock of the good things.

What do you appreciate now, now, now, now, now?

Write.

FIRST THOUGHTS

THE PROPHECY

Make a prediction about your future.

Make it something you want to happen.
Make it something you're going to work hard to make happen.
Make it a prophecy that could change your life.

Is it something you've always wanted?
Or is it a new desire?

Would you have made this same prophecy five years ago?
Ten?
Twenty?

Do you have any hopes and dreams you've given up on?
How do you feel about the evolution of your dreams?

Write.

FIRST THOUGHTS

CASSANDRA

Write a truth someone else didn't believe.

Set the record straight.
If not for them, for yourself.

Write down what you know to be true.
Write down the facts.
Write the hard stuff.
Don't be afraid to let it get messy, ugly, uncomfortable.

Tell the truth.

Write.

FIRST THOUGHTS

PETER

Make a list of your bad habits.

There are things we do when we're younger that we should grow out of. But sometimes it's hard to let those things go.

Write a letter to yourself.
Interrogate yourself about a habit or an attitude you should have outgrown by now.

Tell yourself to grow up.

Write.

BONUS: In his novel *Peter Pan*, J.M. Barrie writes, "All of this has happened before, and it will all happen again." Incorporate the idea of repetition into your writing. How have your bad habits worsened through the passage of time?

FIRST THOUGHTS

THE BOLTER

Are you a bolter?

Spend a few minutes dividing your life into a series of chapters. You decide where each new chapter begins—every new home, every new school, every new job, every breakup, every time you've fallen love. Think of these life-markers as the start of each of your eras. They're all the lives you've lived so far.

Now look through your list.
Did you bolt at the end of any of these chapters?

Examine your history of bolting.
Why did you need to move forward so fast?
Why couldn't you say goodbye?
What were you bolting towards?

Write.

BONUS: Do a deep internet dive into the story of real-life "bolter" Idina Sackville. Explore the various ways you either do or don't identify with Idina's controversial life choices.

FIRST THOUGHTS

ROBIN

Try to remember what it was like to be innocent.

These are lessons of adulthood:
People we trust will betray us.
People we love will let us down.
No one is perfect.
The best we can do is try to be good, and sometimes we will fail.

All these lessons can make us bitter, jaded, wary.

Close your eyes and go back to a time before you knew the world could be cruel.

Paint a picture of that younger you.
How did it feel to see the world through their eyes?
Can you bring any of your youthful innocence back into the present?

Write.

FIRST THOUGHTS

THE MANUSCRIPT

Write what you know.

That's the prompt.
Write what you know.
Everything you know.

What wisdom have you gained in your time so far on this planet?
What do you believe?
What do you have faith in?
And here's a big question: what's the secret of life? (Or, at least, what do you know so far about what it means to be human?)

I know these are big questions. Your answers can be big too! Or small. Think of this as a prompt you can keep coming back to. Think of this as the beginning of your own manuscript. Think of this as a chance to really make sense of your life and why we're all here.

Be vulnerable and earnest.
Embrace your contradictions.
What do you know?

Write.

FIRST THOUGHTS

About the Author

Erik Patterson is an award-winning screenwriter, playwright, and writing teacher.

His play, *One of the Nice Ones*, earned the Los Angeles Drama Critics Circle Award. His theater work has been produced or developed by Playwrights' Arena, the Los Angeles Theatre Centre, Theatre of NOTE, the Evidence Room, The Actors' Gang, the Echo Theater Company, the Lark Play Development Center, Moving Arts, Black Dahlia, Naked Angels, the Mark Taper Forum, and New Group. His plays have been nominated for the Ovation Award, the Stage Raw Award, the LA Weekly Award, and the GLAAD Media Award.

His writing for TV has been recognized with the Humanitas Prize and the Writer's Guild Award, as well as two Emmy nominations. Along with his screenwriting partner, Jessica Scott, Erik has written projects for Warner Bros., Universal, 20th Century Fox, Disney, Freeform, MTV, Paramount, Hallmark, and Syfy, among others. Film and TV credits include: *Abandoned* (starring Emma Roberts and Michael Shannon), *R.L. Stine's The Haunting Hour*, *Another Cinderella Story* (starring Selena Gomez and Jane Lynch), *Deep Blue Sea 2*, *Radio Rebel*, and many more.

Erik is a graduate of Occidental College and the British American Drama Academy. He has developed a wealth of writing prompts through online "Sunday Sprints" that attract writers seeking community and inspiration to do their best work.

www.erikpatterson.org

Books by Erik Patterson

Pop Prompts: 200 Writing Prompts Inspired by Popular Music
Available on Amazon and the TikTok Shop in paperback and e-book

Pop Prompts is a collection of writing prompts that will help you break through creative blocks. Each prompt is paired with a song. Let the music be your muse as you work on your memoir, novel, script, poem—or even your own songs. This book can also be a daily jumpstart for therapeutic journaling. Use it however you want, whenever you want.

Pop Prompts: The '90s
Available on Amazon and the TikTok Shop in paperback and e-book

Pop Prompts: The '90s takes you on a journey through a decade of music that will liberate the writer in you. R&B, rock, rap, grunge, hip-hop, pop, punk. The lines between mainstream vs. counterculture disappeared as musicians embraced the mantra of their time: anything goes. Now it's your turn. Each '90s song in this book is your cue to write with abandon.

Pop Prompts Showtunes
Available on Amazon and the TikTok Shop in paperback and e-book

This unique collection of writing prompts based on American musical theater classics spanning more than 100 years is for anyone ready to discover how showtunes can activate and elevate your writing journey. The book includes a *Fun Home* mini master class. Take a deep dive into Jeanine Tesori and Lisa Kron's brilliant musical. Use the prompts to write a Broadway-bound musical of your own. There is also a High School Edition of *Pop Prompts Showtunes*, with prompts specifically geared towards younger writers—and makes a wonderful teaching companion to English and Drama classes.

Pop Prompts For Swifties Volumes 1 & 2 now available!

If you only have one book in the *Pop Prompts For Swifties* series, make sure to complete your collection of creative journaling prompts inspired by Taylor Swift songs. Both books are available on Amazon and the TikTok Shop in paperback and e-book.

Pop Prompts For Swifties: 99 Writing Prompts
Every writing prompt in this book is paired with one of Taylor's songs from her first five eras. You don't even have to be a Swiftie—anyone can use these prompts for self-expression and reflection. As a bonus, each prompt includes blank journal pages. Put on your favorite Taylor Swift album, pick a prompt, and write!

Includes writing prompts inspired by songs from:
Taylor Swift (2006)
Fearless (2008)
Speak Now (2010)
Red (2012)
1989 (2014)

More Eras: Pop Prompts For Swifties, Volume II
Continue your creative journey of self-expression with 119 new and original writing prompts inspired by the music of Taylor Swift.

Includes writing prompts inspired by songs from:
Reputation (2017)
Lover (2019)
Folklore (2020)
Evermore (2020)
Midnights (2022)
The Tortured Poets Department (2024)

The *Pop Prompts For Swifties* books will get you thinking deeply about yourself, your life, your world—just like Taylor. Use these prompts to write your most personal stories. You know Taylor would...

Your Weekly Writing Sprint

Interested in more writing prompts? Need some motivation? Do you work better when someone is holding you accountable?

Come to YOUR WEEKLY WRITING SPRINT.

I host gently-guided writing sprints on Zoom every Wednesday from 6 to 8 p.m. PST and every Sunday from noon to 2 p.m. PST.

Here's how it works: I give a new writing prompt every fifteen minutes. You write. That's it.

All sprinters stay on mute. Alone but not alone, you can draw creative energy from the community of writers on your screen. This is a fun, low-pressure environment—a safe space for you to experiment with your writing. No worries: I will never ask you to share your work.

You decide how to use this distraction-free writing time. Work on that screenplay, novel, short story, play, poem, song. Do some therapeutic journaling. Write letters to loved ones. Do some technical writing. Create a D&D campaign. Finish your homework. Seriously, whatever you need to work on.

Let's get that writing done. Together.

Join the Your Weekly Writing Sprint Patreon at:
www.patreon.com/erikpatterson

Subscribe to the mailing list at:
www.erikpatterson.org/sundaysprints

www.ingramcontent.com/pod-product-compliance
Lightning Source LLC
Chambersburg PA
CBHW071152130626
46553CB00004B/1626